Herzog & de Meuron Eberswalde Library

Architecture Landscape Urbanism 3:
Eberswalde Library
Herzog & de Meuron

Authors:
Gerhard Mack, Valeria Liebermann

Translations:
Fiona Elliott (Reflections on a
Photographic Medium...), Ishbel Flett
(Building with Images)

AA Publications are initiated by the
Chairman of the Architectural
Association, Mohsen Mostafavi. This
publication has been edited by Pamela
Johnston and designed by Nicola Bailey.
Editorial assistants: Justin McGuirk and
Mark Rappolt.

ISBN 1 902902 08 4

Contents © 2000
Architectural Association and the Authors
AA Publications
36 Bedford Square
London WC1B 3ES
www.aaschool.ac.uk/publications

Printed in Italy by Grafiche Milani

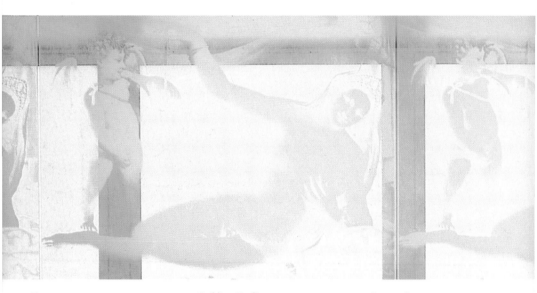

Cover

Detail from Thomas Ruff's portrait of
Eberswalde Library, 1999

Picture Credits

Margherita Spiluttini 2-3, 6, 16, 17, 18,
19, 20, 21, 24, 27, 29, 40–41, 51, 52
Thomas Ruff 14,15, 30, 34–37 (from
archive), 57, 58, 61, 62
Herzog & de Meuron 9–13, 25, 26, 42,
49, 53
Architectural Association Photo Library
46, 47 (Valerie Bennett)
Bildarchiv Preussischer Kulturbesitz
34 bottom
Klaus G. Beyer 36 centre
Ullstein Bilderdienst 45
Thames & Hudson 39 right

Building Credits

Project 1994–96
Built 1997–99

Client: State of Brandenburg
Partners in charge:
 Pierre de Meuron, Harry Gugger
H&deM design team:
 Jacques Herzog, Pierre de Meuron,
 Harry Gugger, Philippe Fürstenberger,
 Andreas Reuter, Katsumi Darbellay,
 Susanne Kleinlein, Yvonne Rudolf,
 Stefan Eicher (model)
Facade design: H&deM in collaboration
 with Thomas Ruff

Construction management:
 Andreas Mayer-Winderlich,Berlin
Structural engineering: GSE, Berlin
Facade planning: Ludwig + Mayer, Berlin
Electrical planning: Ing. Büro Penke,
 Berlin
Climate control/sanitary planning:
 Dörner + Partner, Eberswalde
Physics: Ing. Büro Axel Rahn, Berlin
Acoustics: BesB, Berlin
Glass panels: Fensterwelt, Eberswalde
Concrete panels: Betonsteinwerk Uetze,
 Uetze

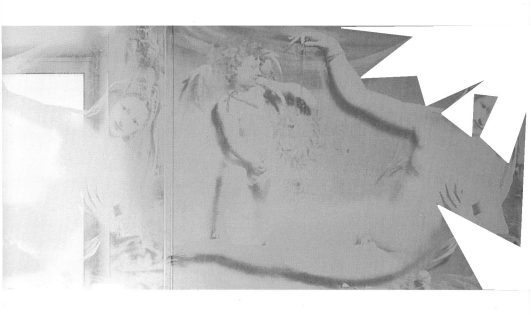

ARCHITECTURAL ASSOCIATION

Herzog & de Meuron

Eberswalde Library

Building with Images
Herzog & de Meuron's
Library at Eberswalde

Gerhard Mack

'It is only shallow people who do not judge
by appearances. The true mystery of the world
is the visible, not the invisible.'
Oscar Wilde, *The Picture of Dorian Gray*

Today's man of the world likes plain shoes and white walls and chooses to
listen to Wagner or Beethoven after the cares of the day – thus spake Adolf
Loos in 1908. But times have changed. Nowadays, a rave has as much appeal
as a classical concert, and white walls are considered rather boring unless, like
a cinema screen, they have images flickering across them. (Indeed, today's
society is so image-oriented that, to make your mark, you must yourself
generate images.) As for footwear, it has become apparent that the plain shoe
needs the foil of the fancy brogue, otherwise the fine quality of its leather
might go unnoticed.

In the fickle world of fashion, only change is always *à la mode*. The avant-
garde striving for innovation has long since given way to the struggle to
devise something new for each coming season. Today's society is geared not
towards growth, but towards differentiation. The latest fad – the width of
stripe on a sweater or a pair of trainers – can confer the modicum of superi-
ority which allows someone to feel that they stand out from the crowd. Social
routines have become a complex charade, moral imperatives a matter of perspective, values more perishable than fresh fruit. Under such circumstances, it
has become conceivable that ornament – criminalized by Loos's 'Ornament
and Crime'[1] – will gain a new lease of life.

Ornament's rehabilitation began with 'post-modernism'. The pattern art
of the late 1970s gave us a foretaste of its acceptance in painting, but the
slumbering debate in architecture has come to life only now, with Herzog &
de Meuron's library for Eberswalde Polytechnic.

View from northwest

Eberswalde Library lies between an overgrown park and a motley collection of small-town architecture (East German style), about an hour's drive north-east of Berlin. From the road the building looms suddenly into view – a massive block that appears to be wrapped entirely in some kind of decorated scaffolding sheeting (rather like the wrapping of Berlin's former royal palace, the Stadtschloss, by the group lobbying for its reconstruction). But first impressions are misleading. On closer inspection, it becomes apparent that the 'sheeting' is in fact the building itself.

A simple cube of concrete and glass panels has been tattooed from top to bottom with a pattern of images – like the body of a Papuan. With no instantly recognizable infrastructure, it stands as a monolith amid the frayed urban fabric – like an object from some distant star, solid yet filigree, definitely alien yet absolutely unresolved, seemingly not quite certain whether it should retain this form or dissolve once more into a *fata Morgana*, conjuring up for the weary traveller a heavenly vision of babbling fountains and beautiful women. Once seduced, the traveller is impaled on the building's knife-edged surfaces. As in Plato's cave, the building evinces the power of the imagination to transform the way we see a structure – a power stronger than truth.

Yet unlike some baseless utopia (that only appeals because it constantly presents a new image) the Eberswalde Library fires our imagination from a firm structural foundation. A concrete core is surrounded by an outer shell of pre-fabricated concrete and glass panels. The panels present a picture plane which at first appears diffuse, then becomes increasingly distinct, until finally it reveals individual motifs and images. Each panel shows a photographic image, and each image is repeated horizontally sixty-six times, like a static film reel. The panels encircle the building in seventeen horizontal bands (although some of the images span several bands). The building is 'framed' by the reiteration of one of the bands at its top and bottom. From a distance, neither the different construction materials nor the sequence of the three floors, with their clerestory windows, can be distinguished. By virtue of its tattooed skin, the concrete block becomes an enclosed entity whose appearance alters with changes in the light and weather. When seen from an acute angle, or in the rain, the images on the concrete seem to become sharper, and the panels begin to resemble lead-type newspaper printing plates. At night, the motifs on the clerestory glazing glow like back-lit urban billboards. In extreme cold or bright light, the motifs on both concrete and glass acquire a sketch-like quality.

The State of Brandenburg commissioned the library, along with a seminar building, in 1994, as part of the post-unification restructuring of the East German educational system. The Forestry Academy of Eberswalde, estab-lished in 1830, was re-founded as a polytechnic in 1992, and its curriculum was revised to encompass courses in forestry, land use and conservation,

Site plan

8

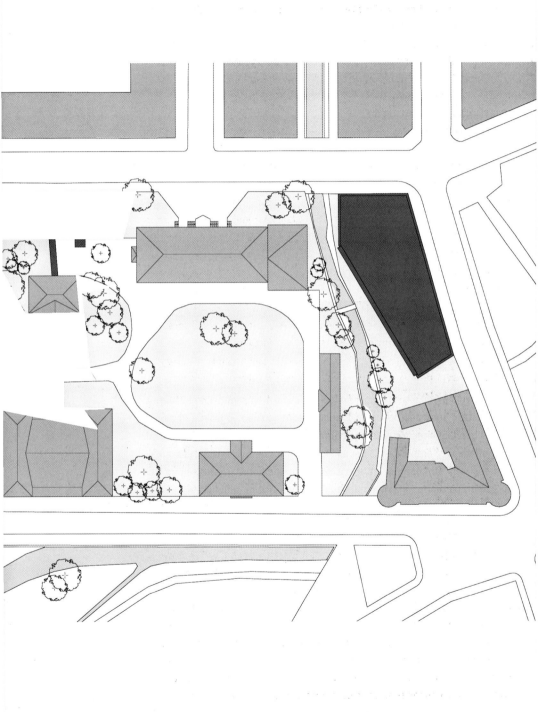

woodworking techniques and business management. An increased capacity – for up to a thousand students from all over Germany – required an improved infrastructure and new facilities. Expansion had hitherto been piecemeal. The school consisted of a disparate group of structures – nineteenth century, twentieth century, pitched-roof, flat roofed, brick, rendered – which were all clustered around a central open area defined by mature trees and a small stream, the Schwärze. As a whole, the trapezoidal campus made little impact on the surrounding streetscape of Eberswalde – itself an undistinguished assemblage of pre-war middle-class houses, bomb sites, GDR blocks and outcrops of Western-style housing from the post-unification period.

Herzog & de Meuron used the heterogeneity of the town and the campus as the starting-point for the project. They placed both of the new buildings in undeveloped corners of the campus, so as to close it off from the town and define its central open area as an autonomous space. Playing on the existing diversity, they designed two solitary buildings which are completely different, but which nevertheless lend a distinctive character to the campus as a whole. The conical seminar building contains a student refectory and a garden café overlooking the river. It is a public building very much in the spirit of classical modernism, clad in brown clinker brick, with large square windows which convey a sense of openness and calm. The library building, on the other hand, is designed as a simple box, and the short corridor that links it to the adjacent book depository and administrative offices (housed in a 1912 building) emphasizes the separateness of the structures rather than bridging the gap between them.

View from east

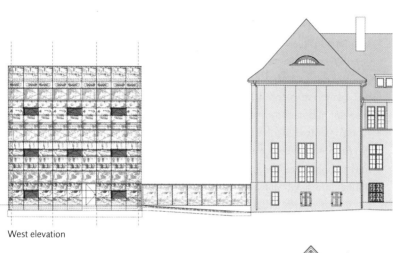

West elevation

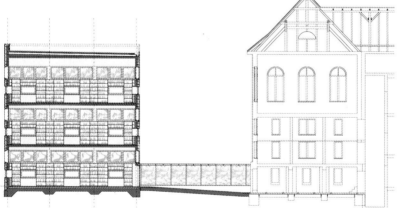

Cross section

Portrait of Eberswalde Library by Thomas Ruff

North facade at night

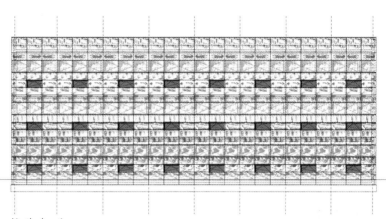

North elevation

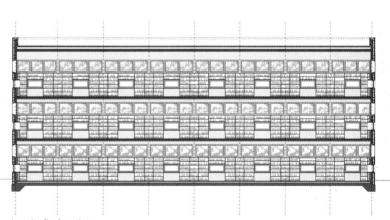

Longitudinal section

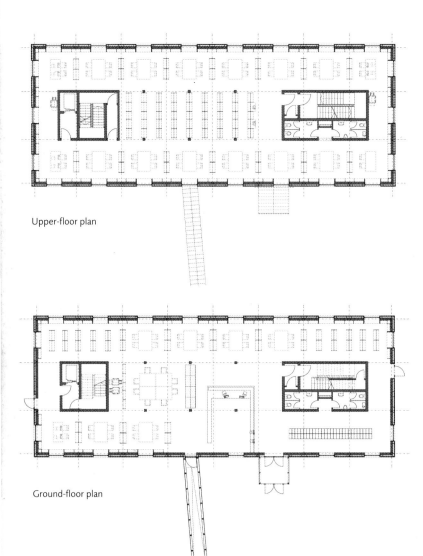

Upper-floor plan

Ground-floor plan

Main entrance on south side

View of north facade

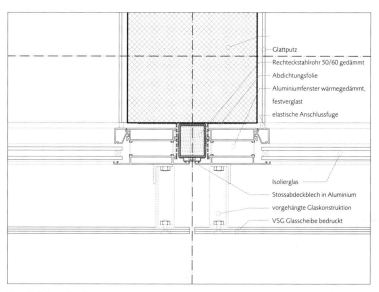

Glattputz
Rechteckstahlrohr 50/60 gedämmt
Abdichtungsfolie
Aluminiumfenster wärmegedämmt,
festverglast
elastische Anschlussfuge

Isolierglas
Stossabdeckblech in Aluminium
vorgehängte Glaskonstruktion
VSG Glasscheibe bedruckt

Detailed plan of sashes

OVERLEAF:
View from east showing glazed
corridor to library administration;
detail of facade

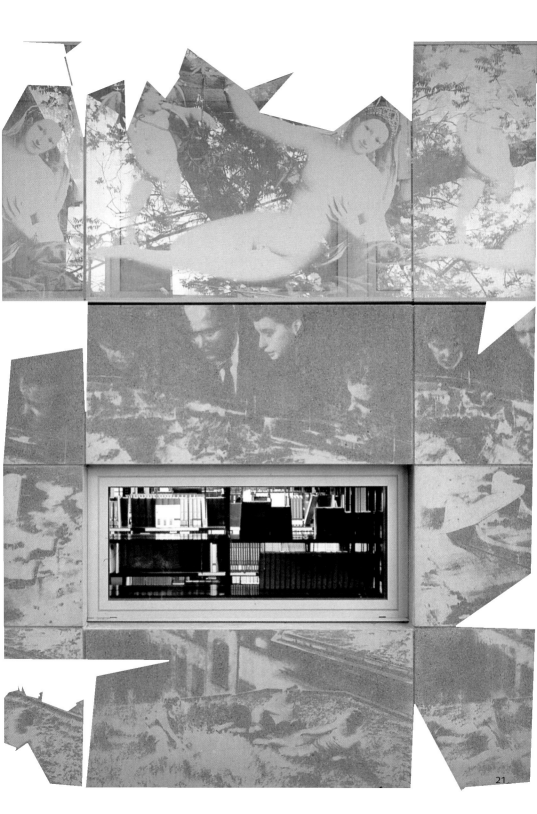

Concrete Sgraffito: Techniques and Origins

While the planning solution for the library is elegant, the printed facade might be described as spectacular. To achieve it, a number of technical difficulties had to be overcome. Printing the glass was relatively simple – the photographs were reproduced using a silk-screen process. However, for the concrete panels, Herzog & de Meuron adapted – and greatly refined – a technique used in the application of simple geometric patterns to prefabricated panels for the DIY market. The photographs are transferred onto a special plastic film by means of a silk-screen process, using a cure-retardant instead of ink. The printed film is then placed into the formwork (taking care to avoid any slip-page) and concrete poured over it. The amount of retardant used controls the degree to which the surface of the concrete sets. When the panel is taken out of the formwork, and carefully washed with water and brushes, the concrete that has lain in contact with the retardant remains liquid and is rinsed away, leaving darker, rougher areas of exposed grey aggregate. The difference be-tween rough and smooth, dark and light, causes the pixelated patterns to emerge as images. The quality of definition depends on the brightness and clarity of the image, and on the contrast between the colours of the wet cement and the aggregate. Weather conditions such as temperature or humidity can also greatly affect the outcome of the process. With the Eberswalde Library, covering the entire building with a variety of repeated motifs and achieving a uniform result was clearly not an easy task.

It is not entirely correct to describe this process as concrete printing. It is, rather, a semi-industrial, semi-manual adaptation of sgraffito, a technique used in Italy and Germany as early as the fourteenth century. The technique reached its zenith in the facade decoration of Italian Renaissance palaces, but examples of the art still grace old farmhouses in Alpine Switzerland, especially in the Grisons region. A dark-coloured plaster is covered in a lighter layer of smooth stucco, into which forms are then scratched, or motifs engraved (floral ornament is particularly popular).

Printing and sgraffito require two fundamentally different approaches. The former is additive, whereas the latter, by scratching or washing out the concrete, injures the surface. In this respect sgraffito addresses the wall's tex-tural qualities to a far greater extent than printing does. It transforms the wall into a complex multi-layered structure whose surface acts like a relief and reflects the light in a very different way to a smooth, printed wall. Such architecture no longer adheres to Le Corbusier's famous definition of 'the masterly, correct and magnificent play of masses brought together in light',[2] but is an outlining of surfaces in light.

It is worth noting that Gottfried Semper, the most important German architect of the Early and High Victorian era, campaigned for a revival of sgraffito techniques.[3] Semper perceived the wall as a textural element added to the supports and the roof at a relatively late stage in construction, and accorded it a largely decorative role in addition to its partitioning function. The sgraffito technique, evoking the art of tattooing, also brings us closer to the human body itself. Herzog & de Meuron repeatedly refer to the building as a body, an attitude akin to that of Renaissance architects who based their buildings on idealized human proportions (a tradition upheld by Le Corbusier's *Modulor* and Buckminster Fuller's search for ideal units of measure-

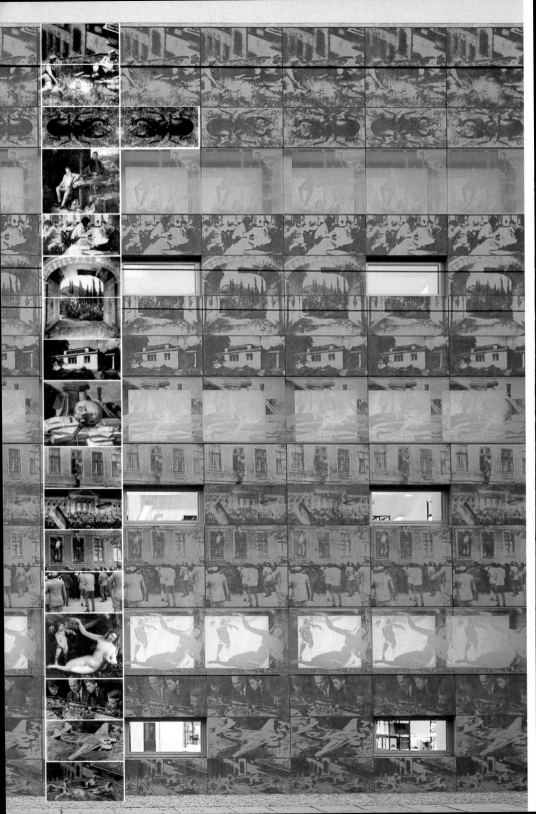

Detail of Eberswalde Library facade highlighting pictorial programme

HERZOG & DE MEURON
Sils-Cuncas, 1991

ment). In the case of the library, however, this affinity is not evoked structurally but is expressed in a more contemporary way, through the surface of the building and its imagery.

Herzog & de Meuron had already experimented with the sgrafitto technique in their competition-winning design for the settlement of Sils-Cuncas in the Upper Engadine. Their intention was to engrave sentences into the plaster facades of a group of varied flat-roofed, cube-shaped buildings, so combining an old technique with a product of the modern age – slogan-making – which has also been adopted by artists such as Lawrence Weiner or Jenny Holzer in a variety of forms (using painted, cast, or even LED – and thus immaterial – text). The bands of lettering, in a sense, took the place once occupied by arabesques. The script – even its content – assumed an ornamental character. The project restored to ornament a symbolic status that it had lost during the nineteenth century. However, it was perhaps too bold for the local population, who rejected it.

A design for a Greek Orthodox church in Zurich (1989) was likewise rejected by the incumbent Bishop. Herzog & de Meuron proposed cladding the inside of the church with translucent marble panels tattooed with images of icons which were held in museum collections and consequently separated from their sacred function. The marble wall was a translucent membrane; during the day it admitted natural light, bathing the entire space in honeyed tones of yellow, whilst at night it screened the lit interior from external view. The Bishop may have sensed that this arrangement was overly humanistic, even though the ornamental motif was reminiscent of older building traditions, such as the tracery of Gothic times. Here the ornament mediated between interior and exterior – it gave structure to the empty aperture,

framed it, shaped it, and made it a focus of interaction. The filtered light evoked a sacred presence far removed from daily life. But the tattooing of the Godhead was evidently too troublesome a notion for His earthly representatives to accept.[4]

Herzog & de Meuron's first opportunity to apply the picture-transfer technique came in 1993, with the Pfaffenholz Sports Centre in St Louis, France (just across the border from Basle). In this cube-shaped building, which is partly sunk below ground level, printed motifs are applied to both the glass and the concrete of the outer skin. On the long side of the building the lower changing room area is clad in concrete panels that have been washed to create flecked biomorphic forms, reminiscent of oversized raindrops – a much freer pattern than the previous geometrical exercises of concrete manufacturers. The pattern visually connects the long wall, cantilevered roof and large forecourt as a single unit. Roof, wall and floor appear to merge into each other and then flow onwards, over the grassy spaces around the building. By virtue of this movement the building opens up and the monolithic materiality of its simple cubic form is dissolved. The fluidity of the surface and the geometry of the volume appear to stimulate our perception in entirely opposite ways. The tattooed skin is both an architectural feature and a (more or less) natural element: it once again transposes the abstract stereometric volume into the plane, and makes it seem all the more like a foreign body on a sports ground. In the Eberswalde Library both the process and the function of this concrete imaging technique have been further refined.

The Box as Autonomous Form

The use of concrete panels to create the library's curtain wall might – naively – be interpreted as a reference to the system building techniques of the former GDR. But it is of greater interest to note its parallels with the architects' earlier works, in which the simple stereometric volume of the cube, or box, constitutes a central theme.

The initial budget for Eberswalde Library was very low, and funding cuts reduced it further. There were similar financial constraints with the Antipodes I student halls of residence for the University of Burgundy in Dijon, designed in collaboration with Rémy Zaugg. Both buildings are simple geometric volumes

HERZOG & DE MEURON
Pfaffenholz Sports Centre,
St Louis, France, 1989–93

with a high proportion of prefabricated components. Both may be described as monoliths that stand as autonomous figures on open ground. (I use the torm figuro with caution, as Herzog & de Meuron do their utmost to avoid figurative traits.) The seven units of the halls of residence are arranged on alternate sides of a circulation spine, to form a linear configuration of repetitive elements that dispenses with the hierarchy of front and rear facades. In the same spirit, the facade of the Eberswalde Library is uniformly covered with panels – a scaly skin. (The absence of panels from the top of the courtyard is not a design choice but an act of compliance with local building regulations on rainwater drainage.) Furthermore, its ornamental character is already foreshadowed in the halls of residence at Dijon, where light prefabricated concrete panels and window elements have been inserted into a black-stained concrete structure, creating a simple serial pattern. At Dijon, however, it is the heaviness of the material that is emphasized, whereas at Eberswalde the building seems to hover weightlessly in space.

For this motif, the Goetz Gallery in a Munich suburb may be seen as a precedent. It is a simple 'box' that seems to float, ethereal as a phantom, amid a stand of birch trees. The exterior can be read either as a plane or as an entire volume. The building's internal division into two floors only becomes apparent when the visitor steps inside: it then emerges that the plinth of glass is a band of clerestory windows on the lower level, whilst the wooden structure between two bands of glass is the upper floor. The compactness of this interaction is reinforced by the assimilation of the different materials. Within the infill section, concrete, glass and even wooden panels are all integrated seamlessly into the load-bearing system. The various kinds of surface – transparent, opaque and reflective – interact with each other and with the surrounding garden in much the same way as a traditional Japanese house, with its walls of rice paper, relates to the external landscape. It is this interaction, far more than the spatial forces, that determines our perception of the building. Herzog & de Meuron originally wanted to accentuate the continual oscillation between surface and space by making the infill section out of birch plywood (a homage to Aalto). This proved to be impracticable, but the same effect is achieved by using standard building materials in unusual ways. At Eberswalde, in turn, it is the unusual use of images that establishes an ambivalence between surface and volume. To explain this, we must take a closer look at the library.

Pictorial Programme

The images for the facade were selected by Thomas Ruff, an internationally renowned Düsseldorf-based artist who has occasionally collaborated with

HERZOG & DE MEURON
Goetz Gallery, Munich,
1989–92

HERZOG & DE MEURON
Antipodes I student halls of
residence, University of
Burgundy, Dijon, 1992

Herzog & de Meuron in the past. Following a training in the Becher School, Ruff has developed his own distinctive approach to photographic work. His subjects include 'nondescript' buildings, such as terraced housing, which he photographs with the kind of care that portrait-painters of old used to reserve for high-ranking individuals. These pictures fragment the everyday world, singling out an element, in frontal perspective, so as to reveal its specificity, its materiality. Paradoxically, it is precisely through the technical reproduction of the picture that the banal subject regains its aura. Ruff's work views the everyday world without preconceptions and recognizes the inherent values of banalized materials, forms and gestures – an approach that can also be found in the work of Herzog & de Meuron (for example in their rehabilitation of unpopular materials such as roofing paper or plywood). Ruff's portraits show the mass products of everyday architecture in all their shabbiness and sadness, but at the same time their subtle composition lends the buildings a surreal touch. There is an overlapping of the banal and the extraordinary, of the functional and the object-like, which challenges our habitual ways of seeing. The same ambivalence and tension characterize buildings by Herzog & de Meuron such as the Frei Photo Studio in Weil am Rhein (1982) or the Plywood House in Basle (1985).

If Thomas Ruff acknowledges the extent to which photographic representation can determine the appearance of a building, then the work of Herzog & de Meuron gives new impetus to the architectural debate. And it is this issue, far more than any formal minimalism, which forms the common ground between the architects and the artist.

For Eberswalde, the architects invited Thomas Ruff to make a selection of newspaper photographs from his own archives. The images had to have a dot screen suitable for transfer onto the panels of the facade. The size of the individual panels was also prescribed (1500 x 715 mm for the concrete and 1500 x 1190 mm for the glass). To Ruff, the alternation of materials suggested that the facade be structured in four thematic groups. For the bands of glass he sel-

THOMAS RUFF
Haus Nr. 12 II, 1989

ected images of paintings, thereby introducing another medium into the work.

The use of newspaper photographs is central to Ruff's work, and before this commission he had already produced a comprehensive body of work in which 'found' images were treated in various ways (although always thematically). He employed the same approach for the library facade, but faced two new factors: the vertical alignment of the individual motifs, and their outdoor location.[5]

The choice of images was never guided by the kind of pseudo-aesthetic whimsy that initial responses to the work have tended to suggest. But nor was it a random selection. Instead, Ruff proceeded from the principle that the library is a public building whose function is 'to store knowledge and make it accessible' and in doing so 'to develop historical and social awareness'. This awareness was projected in the form of specifically chosen extracts from a visual diary, made up of newspaper photographs related to the arts, history, politics and science, that the artist has been compiling since 1981. Most of the images for the Eberswalde Library are taken from the German weekly current affairs magazine, *Die Zeit*, from 1992 to 1993. Arranged in a sequence beginning on the ground level and rising up to the very top of the building, they portray history and science in a sceptical light. The sequence of images is framed, above and below, by a snapshot of 1920s Berlin, showing some young women on a roof garden listening to the radio. At the foot of the building the image establishes an unusual contrast with the stone pavement, whilst at the top it forms an apt transition to the grass-covered roof. Blurring the distinctions between roof and ground, grass and sky, the work also addresses the categories of high and low, which can in turn suggest an engagement with social values such as good or bad, strong or weak.

Above the scene of relaxed modernity, skirting the foot of the building, is the image of an aircraft oddly reminiscent of a flounder. A prototype of the aircraft, known as CBY-3, was developed in Canada but never went into production. The image reminds us that 'progress' can sometimes yield strange results and is not a failsafe path to success or glory. At the same time it may also trigger memories of the Allied air lift that kept Berlin's western sector alive during the Soviet blockade of 1948 to 1949.

The scepticism towards technology is reinforced, in a social context, by the final image in the first grouping: a father and his sons leaning contentedly over a child's model railway. 'They are sitting there like gods, surveying the world they have created – an absurd situation', Ruff has said of the picture, which *Die Zeit* reproduced from the 1964 catalogue of the Märklin model railway company. In the journal the picture bears the anodyne caption, 'When men are enjoying themselves...' but, in this particular context, the idyllic (and quite) fictional family scene has – perhaps unintentionally – acquired real historical connotations. Not only were model railways a favourite plaything of Hermann Goering, Hitler's Reichsmarschall, but, more poignantly, trains transported millions of soldiers and concentration camp victims to their deaths.

If anything can counter the horrors of the past, it is love. On the lowest glass band of the building love appears in the seductive form of Venus, taken from Lorenzo Lotto's painting of *Venus and Cupid* in the Louvre.[6] When the library is brightly lit, the sensuous reclining nude shimmers invitingly towards the people of Eberswalde. But even though the figure of Venus may light a path through the dark hours of history, the image also evokes the Judgement of Paris, which unleashed the Trojan War, or the harrowing verso of the medieval allegory of the world as woman – the angel of death and destruction.

In the second and central section of the pictorial programme the latent motif of violence assumes a historically specific form. Spanning three full panels is a famous photograph taken on 17 June 1961, the day the Berlin Wall went up. In it, we see a seventy-year-old woman being lowered on a rope from her house in Bernauer Strasse into the western sector of the city, while the East German police are already at work bricking up the windows and doors of her building. The crowd of onlookers have their backs turned both to us and to Lorenzo Lotto's Venus. This scene of internecine strife and division created some controversy at the polytechnic. As a compromise, to temper opposition, it was suggested that the image be overlaid with a scene of reconciliation from the days following the toppling of the Wall. This was technically impossible, so Ruff instead incorporated an image of a flag-waving crowd in front of the Berlin Reichstag, positioning it in such a way that it cuts across the feet and lower body of the woman escaping from Bernauer Strasse. The depiction of such patriotic jubilation against the backdrop of a building famously violated by the Nazis maintains a sense of discomfort. A razor-sharp reminder that the new united Germany can only succeed if it preserves the lessons of its past, the photograph also highlights the role played by buildings in that history.

This warning is followed by a *memento mori* – on the second band of clerestory windows, where Ruff has selected a detail from a *vanitas* by Pieter Potter – a still-life of a study table with books and a skull. This melancholy landscape of classical learning is placed within the vertical sequence of images on the library facade, and related to the historical situation in such a way that it can be interpreted as a further exhortation to refer to the lessons of the past to shed light on present-day problems.

The following group of images looks in more detail at the subject of architecture and tertiary education. The Haus am Horn, 61 in Weimar, designed in 1923 by Georg Muche and built by Walter Gropius's practice, is a famous Bauhaus icon – a clean-lined Italianate villa. But above it Ruff has placed the dilapidated arch of a gateway from the Renaissance palace of Colle Ameno in Bologna. He shows us that, for all its *firmitas*, architecture is bound to go the way of everything of this earth. As though this reference to mortality were not enough, Ruff further disrupts the motif by cutting a hole in the archway and inserting into it an idyllic landscape in central perspective. In the context of the Eberswalde Polytechnic, with its emphasis on forestry and timber technology, this may be regarded as a reference to the tension between architecture and nature.

This exterior view is followed by an introspective one, a photograph of students working in the library of the International Atlantic College at St Donat's Castle in South Wales. The introverted intimacy of their study is reversed, and we see the students sitting at their desks as though the wall of the library had been symbolically removed or made transparent. The internal space appears on the outside, and vice versa.

On the upper band, the figure of Humboldt, taken from an 1856 painting by Eduard Ender entitled *Alexander von Humboldt in South America with the Botanical Expert Aimé Bonpland*, takes the theme of research back to an earlier juncture. Whereas the two lower clerestory bands place Love and Death prominently within closed interior settings, the upper band sees the untamed jungle encroaching into the laboratory of the naturalist. Humboldt himself seems somewhat tentative, as if he had more questions than answers. It is hard to imagine him reaching out optimistically to embrace the coming Industrial Revolution. On the contrary, the choice of this picture reinforces the sense of scepticism about the impact of science and technology.

Humboldt's expedition to South America, from 1799 to 1804, was unusual in that it was self-financed and not motivated by political or economic gain. Following his return, Humboldt spent the next two decades in Paris, analysing the material he had gathered and using it to develop a holistic concept of nature in which the individual and the universal are inextricably linked. In the process, he paved the way for new methods of scientific research.

Apparently Humboldt did not particularly like Ender's painting because it depicted the wrong kind of instruments – the scientist's insignia of power, so to speak, were stripped of their authority. The image expresses a critique of scientific empiricism, but it also has a direct connection with the locale – for Humboldt supported, and secured, F. W. L. Pfeil's application to found the Forestry Academy by presenting his case to the Prussian king.

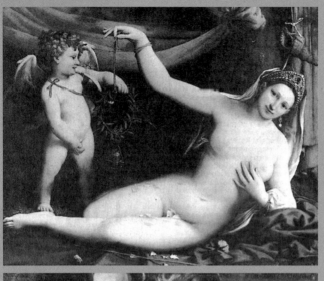

4

3

2

1

15

14

13

The particular character of the locale is also alluded to in the motif immediately below the concluding frieze: pairs of stag beetles turning alternately towards and away from each other (thus avoiding the impression of a herd of insects stampeding around the building). More than any other motif on the library, this sequence of mirror images addresses the issue of ornamentation. Thomas Ruff has spoken of the facade as a 'poster wall' whose lack of structure contrasts with the structure within the ornament. He has referred to his baroque love of imagery and the pleasure he takes in juxtaposing seemingly incompatible images. Herzog & de Meuron, on the other hand, tend to see the building more as an ornamental sign that punctuates the discourse of architectural history, restoring some of the possibilities prohibited by Adolf Loos's brilliant white modernism.7

Evidently, this is a building which plays with – and indeed demands – different ways of seeing. Vertically, as in an ancient Chinese scroll, a programme unfolds before our eyes, charting the stations of a historical narrative – a secular version of a cathedral's stained-glass windows, albeit without the luminous colours. Horizontally, the serial repetition of more dynamic forms and motifs comes together to make an ornamental gesture that locks individual images into a frieze-like movement, encompassing not only the beautiful curve of Venus's back but also the more geometrical forms of the windows on the Bernauer Strasse building and the crowd of people standing around it – not to mention the stag beetles. The viewpoint and the light determine whether it is the continuity of motion or the individual image that predominates. The spectator's gaze determines the fluctuating status of the motif.

One motif in which history and ornament overlap was abandoned following protests by both the polytechnic and the local population. It depicted a baton change by the German women's relay team at the Berlin Olympics in 1936, or, more precisely, the split second when the baton was dropped, the team went out of the race – and the Nazi propaganda machine stalled. Herzog & de Meuron were fascinated by the dynamics of the frieze-like movement in the horizontal sequence. The people of Eberswalde, however, saw the picture as an evocation of the Fascist state and rejected it.

But perhaps the truly provocative aspect of the building lies neither in the choice of images nor in the tattooing of the facade itself, but rather in the viewer's continually shifting perception of the building. Remarkably, this functional building, despite the constraints of the budget, has gained such an aesthetic surplus that it seems to embody a response to the crisis of minimal art. More than any other building by Herzog & de Meuron, the Eberswalde Library belongs to that category of 'specific objects' through which Donald

Judd sought to open up the pictorial space of painting into the real space of the spectator. The eyes and the mind are not allowed to rest. The building is constantly changing its status. Object and building, surface and volume, history and decoration, outside and inside, high and low, stillness and movement, closure and perforation – these are some of the parameters between which the interpretive gaze oscillates.

Provocation: Minimalism and Ornament

Minimalism and ornament, bareness and baroque exuberance, concrete box and field of vision, volume and surface – by combining elements that have long been deemed incompatible, the Eberswalde Library challenges the tradition of modernism. Strictly speaking, it challenges the victorious strand of modernism – derived from cubism – which championed the volume, glorified space, and prevailed over modernism's other lineage – art nouveau – which favoured the surface. Adolf Loos challenged the anaemic ornamentalism of late-nineteenth-century European architecture, comparing it to the pioneering steel-frame construction of the Chicago School. He called for authenticity, validity, reliability, substance, and truth to materials, untainted by illusions or cheap tricks. For models he looked to Roman pragmatism rather than the Renaissance, the neoclassicism of Schinkel rather than the romantic art of Semper. He drew attention to the inherent beauty of materials and demonstrated how it could be spoiled by decorative treatment; in doing so he contrasted the simple products of the true craftsman, firmly rooted in a long tradition, with the embellished products of the artisan. Yet Loos's enthusiasm

WALTER GROPIUS
Fagus Factory, 1911: entrance door handle

MIES VAN DER ROHE
Lake Shore Drive Apartments, Chicago, 1948–51

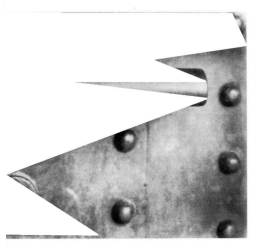

was tempered by a sense that the crafts tradition would be eroded by the very industrialized processes whose functional products he championed.

A similar ambivalence towards ornament permeates classical modern architecture as a whole. Even Gropius, Mies van der Rohe and Le Corbusier, for all their emphasis on the handling of space, did not abandon decorative elements entirely. In Gropius's Fagus Factory there is a detail which famously celebrates the simple stereometric forms that would later become such a central element of Le Corbusier's work – the entrance doors have round handles with rectangular fixings and, at their point of juncture, the circle merges into the rectangle. Moreover, the geometric simplicity of this ironmongery finds its ornamental complement in the three rows of studs which fix overlapping metal panels to the leaf of the door – geometric ornament.

Mies van der Rohe, inventor of the 'building-as-box', was also able to mine ornamental qualities from the material cult of modernism, albeit by other means. This can be seen in his choice of bronze for the non-structural elements in the facade of the Seagram Building in New York – the material's velvety darkness generates a non-functional, purely aesthetic (and therefore

HERZOG & DE MEURON
Storage facility for the Ricola
Factory, Laufen, 1986–87

surplus) effect. Similarly, in an earlier key project, the Lake Shore Drive Apartments in Chicago, he suspended slender steel rods in front of the glass facade, so as to define a distinct extended space (in a manner echoed, many years later, by the layered formwork of Herzog & de Meuron's Ricola storage facility in Laufen). Simultaneously a space and a surface, the interface between the building and the outside world acquires a certain autonomy, a three-dimensionality that structures the three-dimensional building itself. In terms of both function and imagery, the facade fulfils the role traditionally assigned to ornament and decoration.

Le Corbusier, for his part, attached great importance to the role of artworks in decorating a space and developing its full impact, as evidenced by his dispute with the client for the Villa La Roche in Paris, completed in 1923.

Ornament's functional role and its capacity to ensure spatial fluidity were well known to the early exponents of classical modernism. The triumph of steel-frame construction had, after all, already separated the facade from the structure. When J. J. P. Oud used ornamental elements on the facade of Shell's new headquarters at The Hague in 1948, he was accused (by Philip Johnson,

41

HERZOG & DE MEURON
Two libraries, University of
Jussieu, Paris, 1992

among others) of trying to revive ornament and decoration in a structurally arid architecture. In his defence, Oud retorted 'Ornament emphasizes the meaning of the building. It is designed for the light itself and is an aesthetic necessity.'[8]

However, decoration and ornament were only truly reappraised with the advent of pop culture and the commercial trivialization of modernism in the United States. In the early 1960s Robert Venturi divided buildings into a volume and a facade, the former being simple, the latter more considered.[9] The facade, he said, was not a deception which belied the integrity of the building's structure and space. Rather, it was the means by which the building presented itself to the city, to the street and to passers-by. It transformed the building from a monolithic entity into an act of communication – a symbol, a message-bearer. Consequently, the facade was to be designed as an autonomous 'information board' that might have little or nothing to do with the structure of the building itself. Venturi challenged the primacy of modernism's pure stereometric forms. He provocatively compared the 'decorated shed' – representing his concept of architecture as symbolic communication – to the 'duck' – the building shaped by its function.

In conversation, Jacques Herzog has acknowledged Venturi's influence on the development of Herzog & de Meuron's own architectural discourse.[10]

Both share the notion of architecture as an act of communication, embodied not by sterile, fixed forms that can be easily represented by white cardboard models but rather by a constantly oscillating field of perception. Both have an interest in materials and forms that have become so commonplace that people hardly notice them any more. However, Herzog & de Meuron's buildings are not boxes with display frontages in the manner of highway billboards or the Las Vegas Strip – or indeed of Venturi's own proposal (of 1967) for the National Football Hall of Fame in New Jersey. Their facades are more gestural than symbolic in character – even when they convey information.

Take, for example, their competition design for two libraries for the University of Jussieu in the centre of Paris. The scheme envisages a modular, cohesive structure that orders the separate buildings around internal courtyards in a diverse yet fluid manner, so as to create distinct public and private areas. The main facade, overlooking an open square, combines elements of picture and text. As at the Eberswalde Library a central theme is the importance of learning, and of the library in particular as the place in which students will acquire much of the knowledge they will need in their dealings with the world. This is indicated by glass panels onto which portraits of writers and scientists have been screen-printed, and by electronic screens that display quotations from works within the holdings of the two libraries. The two contrasting elements alternate like the layers of a cake. Whereas the portraits are static, animated at most by changes in the lighting of the rooms behind them, the electronic displays are constantly moving in a manner also found in the work of artists such as Jenny Holzer. In keeping with their medium, the quotations fluctuate – they are sometimes complete, sometimes truncated. If the pictures represent continuity, the words convey the passage of time and the cycle of temporal phases.

This allusion to time clearly distinguishes the Jussieu facade from the billboard-style designs that Venturi had in mind in his polemical attack on an ossified modernism. The facade, in Herzog & de Meuron's work, evidently serves to direct the building's character, function, social context and public status. Its intellectual content surpasses that of any commercial sign. Above all, however, its ornamentation is treated in a comprehensive manner that takes it far beyond overt symbolism. The series of portraits on the libraries, for which the architects hoped to commission Gerhard Richter, are arranged in accordance with a basic principle of modernism: serial alignment. One face succeeds another over eight rows. The interposed bands of lettering underscore this simple ornamental trait. The facade can be seen as an 'all-over' consisting of a large number of stylized elements arranged in seemingly endless variations.

This repetition destroys the image in a manner a little reminiscent of Andy Warhol's manipulation of media imagery. Venturi wants to present intact images – he thinks figuratively. Herzog & de Meuron, on the other hand, use images as a building material to other ends. (This sets them apart, moreover, from Jean Nouvel and Rem Koolhaas. For those architects, pop art is still a theme, whereas for Herzog & de Meuron, it is a strategy, an attitude.) Their approach is informed, in a self-evident way, by a constructive spirit. The irony, even cynicism, apparent in Venturi's designs has no place in their work, for the simple reason that it would destroy the homogeneity of visual phenomena that their phenomenological approach demands.

Accordingly, ornament is understood by Herzog & de Meuron in functional terms, as a means of expressing today's realm of experience. The temporal modes of continuity and cyclical movement, reflected in the self-contained, non-functional pattern of the ornamentation, are characteristic of the prevailing perception of time in our society. There is no reference to the linear model of time, in contrast to the avant-garde works of modernism, which strove to improve prevailing conditions, ideally by promulgating Friedrich Schiller's 'aesthetic education' – or, failing that, by observing the principle of constant invention and improvement. There is no place today for such a progressive, dogmatic dialectic. Despite globalization, the grand ideologies have faded. Finality – which implicitly contains the notion of the ineluctable, of man's mortality – is out.

This historical development allows us to look anew at ornament. It indicates that the ornamental tradition comes into its own whenever the idea of linear progress is challenged. In abstract expressionism, Jackson Pollock's *All-Overs* and *Circles* are prime examples of this, as are the cyclical problems of language in Allen Ginsberg's *Howl*, the music of John Cage, and the choreography of Merce Cunningham. In this work it is the persistence of the moment that counts, the creation of the present, the awareness of the fragment, of the arabesque, or even of the ornament. The path towards the acceptance of ornament was prepared by the great dance revues of the 1920s, whose choreography transformed the performers into moving ornaments – three-dimensional formations distinct from the space in which they moved.

Yet architecture found it considerably harder than the other arts to rehabilitate ornament. As a discipline, it was much more closely bound by social factors and, as the boom in low-income housing showed, it was also committed to notions of social improvement. To put it bluntly, architecture had, on principle, nothing to gain from ornament. Ornament was equated with self-satisfaction, which was construed by some – for example, Siegfried

Kracauer in *The Mass Ornament* – as an indication of ingenuousness (a suspicion apparently confirmed by the mass pageantry of Nazi Party rallies). Ornament only acquired a new function once society as a whole shifted away from linear models (as described by Francis Fukuyama in his *End of History*, or by Niklas Luhmann in his virtuoso reflections on self-reference and differentiation) and, through a mix of words and images, attempted to understand time cyclically. The accusation that used to be levelled at ornament – that it was deceit, presenting a false idea of the workings of the structural system, the spatial axes, etc. – might actually be seen as an indication of strength at a time when social interaction is determined by simulation – by cosmetics, trick images and the projection of multiple personalities. When reality is experienced primarily at an aesthetic level, ornament becomes a means of experience.[11]

In the Jussieu project we encounter a more classical variation on the functional use of ornament. The main facade is linked with that of Jean Nouvel's Institut du Monde Arabe via a square that adjoins both buildings. The square fields of photographic shutters on the exterior of the Nouvel building, together with the white marble panels in the interior, are a Western translation of the mushrabeyeh screens and open-walled architecture of the Middle East. They also acknowledge an element of time – for the shutter apertures (when they work) automatically respond to lighting conditions and the passage of the day, shielding the offices, libraries and exhibition spaces from excessive light. It is this response to light, together with the fastness of the metal, that determines the facade. The ornament is traditional in that it has

Girls rehearsing for a Paris dance revue, 1929

a homogenous, all-over pattern, but it also has a certain technical or futuristic aspect: its impact derives from the fact that it contains no further imagery, no inner dynamic generated by a diverse structuring, no interplay between transparency and opacity (unlike the facade of Herzog & de Meuron's project), and not even the merest suggestion of corporeality. It embodies the confrontation between an Eastern approach, seen through Western eyes, and a provocatively contemporary Western approach.

A separate essay would be required to discuss how this contemporary approach relates in any deeper sense to Islamic architecture. Briefly, however, it can be pointed out that the ban on representational art, derived from the Old Testament, not only encouraged the lavish development of ornamental forms in Islamic culture but also informed the communion with the divine, as expressed in traditional architecture. Allah cannot be seen or touched but can only be reached aurally, through the invocation of prayer. Visually, His presence can only be suggested indirectly, by the perfect abstraction of ornamental forms. These create, in the Islamic architecture of light and shadow, a kind of 'negative space' in which the absent deity can be sensed. Yet the built ornament remains a very human work – it encloses an indivisible and sacred space so as to bring it within man's reach whilst at the same time maintaining a sense of openness through the device of perforation. It belongs to the earthly world. The truly divine, on the other hand, is to be found in the original, raw, unworked stone, which remains intact and free of human intervention. This interaction between a volume and the surface that both conceals and reveals it, renders it both immaterial and tangible, is the defining element of traditional Islamic architecture. It can also be found – as a phenomenological structure, without any religious implications – at the heart of many of Herzog & de Meuron's projects.

The repeated references to the facade as a 'pictorial skin' – in the descriptions of the Jussieu project, the library at Eberswalde and other buildings – may also be viewed as a reassertion of ornament's 'worldly' character. After all, the tattooed human body is widely regarded as the primary locus of ornament. In the bourgeois nineteenth century, however, tattooing was driven underground, stigmatized.[12] For Adolf Loos it became an epithet to belittle art nouveau facade designs: the colourful floral ornamentation of Otto Wagner's Majolica House in Vienna (1898/99), for example, was 'tattooed architecture'. When Herzog & de Meuron talk about the facades of buildings such as the Eberswalde Library as being tattooed, they effectively overturn this pejorative evaluation.

Image and Wall

But talking about ornament is not the same as striving towards its rehabilitation. Herzog & de Meuron are not interested in applying pictures to walls by the traditional means of murals or huge canvases. They do not wish to use a decorative facade to pep up a simple stereometric volume. Nor do they see themselves as champions of particular technical processes. It would hardly have occurred to them, for example, to elevate the transfer of photographs onto concrete to the status of a design concept (as concrete manufacturers have been doing ever since the Eberswalde Library opened).[13] Those who

OTTO WAGNER
Majolica House, Vienna
1898–99

reproach Herzog & de Meuron, saying it is old hat to cover facades with ornament, screen-print glass, or incorporate photographs into the architecture, appear to be perpetuating the positivist tradition of evaluating cultural phenomena merely in terms of provenance. But this is not a question of design, nor one of technical process. It is a question of architecture.

In the work of Herzog & de Meuron, the use of ornament should be viewed in the context of a broader investigation into ways of defining the fundamental issues of architecture in a contemporary manner. The different methods of printing and other means of treating the surface are all part of a spatial concept which, as it were, turns the skin of a building inside out, opening up walls and dissolving the structural mass. This distinguishes the work of Herzog & de Meuron from that of other representatives (or perhaps more aptly, 'signature soloists') of the New Swiss–German Architecture.[14] Peter Zumthor, for example, in his Bregenz Arts Centre, uses all means possible to emphasize the space itself. The entire building is an almost religious apotheosis of space, addressing – to use Heideggerian terms – the essence or nature (*Wesen*) of things, and their being (*Sein*), but not their presence or being-in-the-world (*Dasein*). Herzog & de Meuron attempt to achieve the opposite. In situating their buildings they bring the language of architecture to the apex of phenomenology. Rather than asking what a volume or a wall is, they question our ideas and expectations in relation to a volume or a wall. Correspondingly, they define the categories of architecture as categories of perception, which allows them to situate their buildings astride the borderline of hitherto separate concepts. The library at Eberswalde is both a concrete cube and a pictorial skin – at the same time stereometric and planar, monolithic and alive like a tattooed body. The minimalist volume disturbs the images, the images blur the volume. The concrete panels are heavy, the images almost immaterial.

The ambivalence between lightness and heaviness can also be found in a number of Herzog & de Meuron's other projects. Their design for the Grothe Collection in Bonn consists of a concrete volume, with very few openings, whose appearance can be altered by flowing rainwater. When the outer walls are wet they become as smooth as a mirror, and the windows seem to float like the flotsam and jetsam of a shipwreck. The concrete block is transformed into an aquarium; firmness turns into fluidity; the impermeable becomes transparent. In dry weather, however, the building becomes a rock with moss-covered sides – irrefutably massive and stable. In this respect the project is similar to the stone towers proposed by the architects as part of a 1990 ideas competition for redeveloping the centre of Berlin, or the copper-banded signal box in Basle, which is alternately a compact monolith and a delicate

HERZOG & DE MEURON
Art Box: Museum for the
Grothe Collection, Bonn
1996–97

plane, according to the light and the weather. The architecture provides a point of intersection between mass and its sublimation in imagery and thought, between immateriality and its reification. It allows apparent opposites to be seamlessly united – or parted again, at the whim of the weather god.

Though the Grothe project remained unbuilt, an earlier design of 1993 – the Ricola Factory in Mulhouse – implemented the same concept, albeit using different materials. Here, flowing rainwater transforms the two narrow ends of black-stained concrete into seemingly transparent planes that may be equated with the translucent facades along the sides of the building. The latter are made up of printed polycarbonate panels which admit filtered light into the production halls. Depending on the intensity of the light the walls are either closed and compact, or translucent membranes. They are at the mercy of the light. There are elements here from Herzog & de Meuron's design for the Greek Orthodox church in Zurich. The polycarbonate panels offer the same protection as a traditional wall while keeping the transition between interior and exterior as flexible as it would be with a curtain – a concept that Herzog & de Meuron realized in 1998 (in collaboration with artists Rosemarie Trockel and Adrian Schiess) in their marketing building for Ricola in Laufen. Similarly, the wall of the storage facility in Mulhouse is constantly changing in appearance and, in a way, becomes a function of nature. The fact that it

49

incorporates a motif based on a Karl Blossfeldt photograph of a leaf adds a further dimension to this exchange: the wall which confronts nature is composed of an image from nature.

HERZOG & DE MEURON
Stone House, Tavole, 1985–88

Such artifice, ultimately, is what matters to Herzog & de Meuron. Buckminster Fuller once said that he wanted to build houses that were as light as the pictures made of them, and the Basle architects come closer than anyone else today to fulfilling this ideal. By using pictures as a building material they undermine the traditional categories of architecture. This can be seen in their original proposal for the interior of the Eberswalde Library. The three open floors were designed as a wooden container – a warm lining to offset the stern architecture of the exterior. The timber-clad walls were to have wooden bookshelves running around them, an effect not dissimilar to the facade of the Ricola storage facility in Laufen, in terms of its independent spatiality and its transposition, into the interior, of an ambivalence between image and body, surface and volume. The students at their desks would have seen these walls of books as pictorial planes, similar to those shown in Candida Höfer's or Andreas Gursky's photographs of library reading rooms. Picture windows would have been set into the walls in front of the workstations, so as to frame the outside world. One picture would have delineated the other, making it difficult to distinguish what was real and what was artificial, what was close and what was far away. As the exterior and the interior merged, space would have become porous – dissolving and reforming itself in a continual movement.

HERZOG & DE MEURON
Rossetti Hospital Pharmacy,
Basle, 1995–98

Unfortunately, however, this concept for the interior fell victim to a cost-cutting exercise by the Brandenburg government, and the library is now furnished with catalogue products that are scarcely in keeping with the design of the facade. The sense of spaciousness was also sacrificed to economy, which dictated that the two staircores should be linked by floor joists and placed in a self-contained unit at the narrow end of the ground floor. The addition of two rows of columns subdivided the space still further. The generosity of the original space has been eroded, yet an element of intimacy remains, in the form of the soft clerestory lighting which ties together the different floors (as it does in the Goetz Museum in Munich). The library's deeply recessed windows still offer open views, while the ultramarine carpet adds a vibrant note – and a slightly artificial ambience – to the warm-grey rooms.

The interaction between interior and exterior, between volume and surface – which in the library is necessarily restricted to the external facade – has been explored by Herzog & de Meuron in a number of other projects, which can only be outlined here.

In the Blue House (1980), an early work in a Basle suburb, colour is

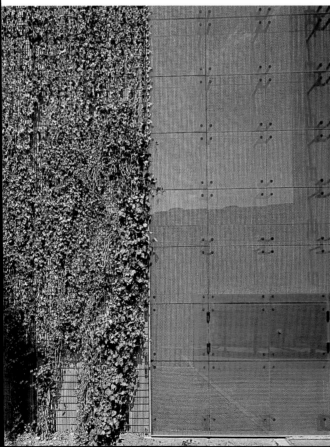

understood as an independent layer detached from the rendered facade – as a picture plane in the spirit of Yves Klein's blue monochrome paintings. It is a skin of colour, a surface coat of paint, yet its powdery texture lends it an independent spatial dimension which makes the building appear light, almost immaterial. Some time later the architects applied rubble to the concrete skeleton of a house in the Ligurian village of Tavole and treated the resultant surfaces as pictures (in the spirit of Leonardo da Vinci, who recommended that old walls should be regarded as pictorial structures). In that project the structural elements were used, almost programmatically, to create a kind of frame that encloses the 'picture walls'. A more traditional form of picture wall can be seen in the proposal for the Greek Orthodox church in Zurich, with its marble panels printed with images of icons. Printed glass panels were used for the first time in the SUVA buildings in Basle (1988–93), where panels bearing the company name unite the old and new parts of the complex behind a single facade, and define a clearer orientation towards the corner of

HERZOG & DE MEURON
Dominus Winery, Napa
Valley, California, 1995–97

HERZOG & DE MEURON
Kramlich Residence and
Media Collection, Napa
Valley, California, 1999–2001:
south elevation and ground-
floor plan

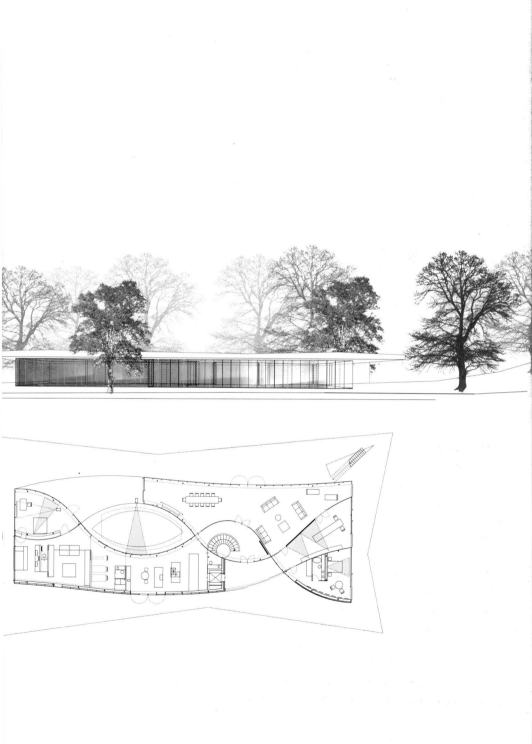

the site. The bottle-green printed glass facade of the Rossetti Hospital Pharmacy in Basle (1995–98) contrasts with areas that are overgrown with ivy, creating a strange interaction whereby the plants appear artificial and the glass appears natural, while the building itself takes on the appearance of a vast aquarium. The earlier Pfaffenholz Sports Centre in St Louis, France (1989–93) sets reality and illusion in flux in a similar manner. In this instance the pattern of the insulation boards is printed onto the inside of the glass panels on the front, extending up to the point where the wall becomes a band of glass. The wall, confronted by its own image, eventually withdraws into the image. Alternatively, a wall might be set in motion by electronic displays and images, as is the case with the libraries at Jussieu (1992). Or it might be porous, an image in itself, as in the very different projects in Napa Valley, California: the Dominus Winery (1995–97) or the Kramlich Residence and Media Collection (1999–2001).

The 100-metre-long winery is integrated into the linear pattern of the vineyards. Its outside walls are made up of a metal grating filled with stones that are densely or loosely packed (depending on the insulation requirements of the interior), with the result that some parts of the building receive no daylight, while other parts receive a good deal. The transparency of the walls is constantly changing.

In the Kramlich Residence, the walls become the vehicle for the pictures. Built for a couple who collect video art, the house consists of several distinct elements. The ground floor, covered by a structurally autonomous roof, is conceived as an open and fluid space. The walls are waved and made of glass. They overlap to form different zones and, in contrast to the solid roof, seem to dissolve the volume into almost pure transparency. They can be negated, only to appear once more; they can form the skin of the facade one minute, an interior wall the next. This variable opacity allows the walls to be both a mirror in which the landscape of Napa Valley is refracted, and a projection screen for video art. In the central axis the walls form display cases. Interior and exterior are no longer deployed for pictorial contrast but form a visual continuity. At the same time, real and fictive worlds interact and, almost imperceptibly, the status of reality changes, giving rise to purely visual intermediate zones reminiscent of the semi-transparent reflections in Dan Graham's pavilions. Through subtle shifts in its status, a single wall can permit entirely different perceptions of space. In this 'landing place' (to use an earlier expression of Herzog & de Meuron) the various levels come together: image, beauty, and ornament, once supposedly superfluous, now return to centre stage. Viewed from the inside, nature appears to be as artificial as the video images that are visible from the outside at night (when they also appear to form the material from which the house is built). The time-honoured principle of *venustas* (delight) defines this architecture. Without it there would be no commodity and no firmness here. The house's walls of glass, unlike those in Mies van der Rohe's famous Farnsworth House in Plano, Illinois, have a load-bearing function. The material appears to dissolve into the kind of immateriality that characterizes the works of video artists such as Bill Viola, Gary Hill and Matthew Barney, which the clients collect and show. The house – itself, in a sense, virtual – is integral to the installation of this new media work. Its rooms generate and are generated by images, akin to the Eberswalde Library – only lighter, faster, more fragile. Here, it is the image that is the true, the ultimate reality. But it too can disappear, leaving only traces in memory, thoughts. An architecture of images, for images.

NOTES

1   Reprinted in Adolf Loos, *Trotzdem. Gesammelte Schriften 1900–1930* (Vienna 1982), p. 78ff (first edition 1931).
2   Le Corbusier, *Towards a New Architecture*, trans. Frederick Etchells (London 1927).
3   Gottfried Semper, *Die vier Elemente der Baukunst* (Braunschweig 1851).
4   C.f. the assessment of Jeffrey Kipnis, who described the ornamental character of Herzog & de Meuron's work as 'a fixation with the cosmetic', in *El Croquis*, no. 84, p. 22ff.
5   All direct or indirect quotes are derived from a conversation between the author and Thomas Ruff in the artist's Düsseldorf studio on 2 July 1999.
6   For information about the provenance of the artworks reproduced in the newspaper images, I am indebted to Frau Annerose Bauer, the now retired Head Librarian at Eberswalde Polytechnic.
7   Pierre de Meuron emphasized this point in the talk he gave at the opening of the library in April 1999.
8   Quoted by Giorgio Grassi in 'On the Question of Decoration' in Demetri Porphyrios, *Building and Rational Architecture*, Architectural Design, nos. 5/6, 1984.
9   Robert Venturi, *Complexity and Contradiction in Architecture* (New York 1977), and later R. Venturi, Denise Scott Brown, Steven Izenour, *Learning from Las Vegas* (Cambridge MA 1978).
10 Herzog & de Meuron in conversation with Jeffrey Kipnis, *El Croquis*, no. 84, 1997, p. 19.
11 Compare, for example, Dan Graham's early works for public spaces in the United States.
12 See Stephan Oettermann's inspired study, *Zeichen auf der Haut, Die Geschichte der Tätowierung in Europa* (Frankfurt 1979).
13 C.f. *Baumeister*, no. 8, 1999, p. 67.
14 Hans Frei has written provocatively on this theme in *Archithese*, no. 2, 1998, p. 62ff, 'Ein Nachruf auf die Neuere Deutschschweizer Architektur'.

'Reflections on a Photographic Medium', 'Memorial to the Unknown Photographer', or 'Visual Diary'? Thomas Ruff's Newspaper Photos

Valeria Liebermann

When Herzog & de Meuron engaged the Düsseldorf artist Thomas Ruff to work on the design for the facade of the Eberswalde Library, they presented him with a precise set of specifications. The building – a simple box – was to be clad all over in printed panels, arranged systematically in clear horizontal and vertical rows. Once both the size and the material of the panels had been decided, Ruff was asked to choose motifs from his *Newspaper Photos* series that could be applied in continuous bands around the facade.[1]

Newspaper Photo 289, 1991: C-Print, 40 x 24 cm

Was the architects' decision to involve Ruff in the design of the facade a purely technical one, in that the newspaper photos, with their dot screen, would transfer well to concrete or glass? Or was it a matter of aesthetics, in that the individual printed concrete panels would look very much like the old printing plates that were once used in newspaper production? Or was it, even, that the artistic concept behind the *Newspaper Photos* series was particularly suited to the free thinking with which libraries are associated?

The images in the series are drawn from an archive of over 2,500 newspaper photographs that Ruff has been assembling since 1981. Although Ruff's primary intention was to document the range of possibilities in contemporary photo-portraiture,[2] over the years he has built up a visual library that spans the full spectrum of the press and illustrates themes in politics, business, culture, science, technology, history and current affairs. However, he selects the photographs not because of their contemporary relevance, but rather because he finds them interesting, strange or absurd in themselves, or because they conform to certain clichés or stereotypes. He does not comb through the newspapers in a methodical way, but simply keeps whatever attracts him at a particular moment. This subjective and somewhat haphazard process of selection means that the archive is not so much a scholarly record of published opinions as it is a visual diary of Ruff's personal response to newspapers as a medium (albeit a diary without words, because from the outset he separated the photographs from the text that went with them).

In 1990 Ruff became aware of the artistic potential of this 'visual diary',[3] and started to experiment. He had already used found material in his *Sterne* series;[4] now he decided to reproduce some of the motifs from his newspaper collection, enlarging them by two hundred per cent, framing them like prints with a broad passe-partout, and then removing any remaining text or captions, so that the individual images could be received and understood 'purely' as pictures. These interventions radically altered the context of the photographs, and raised important questions regarding the role of press photography and our attitudes towards it.

With very few exceptions, the newspaper photographs collected by Ruff were not conceived to satisfy aesthetic or artistic impulses; they simply documented an event in the news. Newspaper photographs must not only be subsidiary to the text; they must also represent its content as lucidly and precisely as possible. Their effectiveness is largely determined by their 'news value', that is to say, by their apparent ability to bring together an event, the depiction of that event, and the text interpreting it (which has nothing to do with the subtlety or the harmony of their composition). With this medium the photographer is often reduced to the status of anonymous journeyman – it is the picture editor who selects the images and decides which aspects of them are important. Often the images are heavily cropped, to fit the layout, or are even retouched, to stimulate interest in the article.[5] However, readers rarely subject such images to critical examination. Unaware that the views presented to them are certainly filtered, perhaps even manipulated, they tend to have an almost naive faith in the truthfulness of the pictorial message.

Ruff long ago abandoned the notion that a photographic image is by definition real or true to life,[6] or that it has intrinsic documentary value or 'objectivity'. For him every photograph is, in the first instance, simply a surface that operates somewhat like a mirror – the viewer usually only sees that which corresponds to his or her own experiences and ideas, and often fails to recognize the photographer's contribution. Consequently, Ruff's visual investigations always circle around the possibilities of photographic techniques – the questions of how a picture comes into being, and how it is perceived.[7]

When it came to selecting individual motifs for his *Newspaper Photos*, Ruff was not at all interested in the content of the articles they had illustrated, or in the relationship between text and image. Rather, he was concerned to find out whether, and how, these photographs could be perceived as pictures in their own right, and whether they would somehow continue to mediate information even after they had been detached from their original context. By doubling the format and removing the captions, Ruff draws greater attention to the composition and the subject-matter of the pictures. Their 'news value' is lost, to be sure, but their intrinsic appeal is regained – certain three-dimensional,

'painterly' qualities, otherwise suppressed by the picture editors' rough hand- *Newspaper Photo* 021, 1990:
ling, re-emerge. And it is precisely these qualities that Ruff wishes to honour C-Print, 16 x 19.5 cm
and restore, as though creating a 'Memorial to the Unknown Photographer'.[8]

Besides focusing on the function of the photographs, Ruff also wants to
lay bare the technical processes, the manner of reproduction, and the results
that ensue. Doubling the format allows him to heighten the impact of the dot
screen, which makes the newspaper photograph instantly recognizable as a
reproduced image. By re-photographing these reproductions, Ruff reinstates
their original surface quality without disguising their function as newsprint
images. In addition he frames these 'reproductions' like fine prints and hangs
them so that they cover an entire wall, in the manner of a nineteenth-century
salon. By pursuing this method, involving double and triple reproductions,
Ruff is engaging in the dialogue surrounding the aura of the 'original'. He
shows clearly that Walter Benjamin's concept of the aura no longer holds true,
now that our pictorial world and our visual thinking are largely defined by the
ubiquitous use of reproductions in the modern media.[9] By the very act of
reproducing newspaper photographs (which are not seen by the viewer in
their original state) Ruff dissembles the hierarchical relationship between
original and reproduction.

Hans-Peter Feldmann was already addressing this issue in the late 1960s,
with results not unlike Thomas Ruff's. His 'Notebooks', bound in grey card
and published in editions of one thousand, consist of uncaptioned illustrations
reproduced from journals, posters and postcards.[10] He would also look in
different newspapers for photographs that were identical, except in terms of
their size and cropping, and present them side by side. In contrast to Ruff,
however, Feldmann pursued the principle of reproduction to extremes,
processing any found, reproduced material, regardless of its source or quality.
He was less interested in the images' content, artistic merit or relationship to
reality than he was in his own critical, subversive exploitation of the pictorial
medium. In light of Feldmann's work, which effectively revised Benjamin's
thesis regarding the aura of the work of art, Ruff has moved on from the
question of what happens to the original during the reproduction process, to
concentrate on the validity of press photographs as images in their own right.

In responding to Herzog & de Meuron's brief for the library, Ruff has
invested the *Newspaper Photos* series with a new dimension. Each individual
photograph, in multiple reproductions, once again becomes a mass-product.
Yet at the same time the various motifs, which were not particularly
emphasized in the original series, are now scrutinized as much for their
pictorial content as for their visual qualities.

After Ruff had accepted the commission, he started by asking himself
what a library is, and what function it has. He came to the obvious conclusion

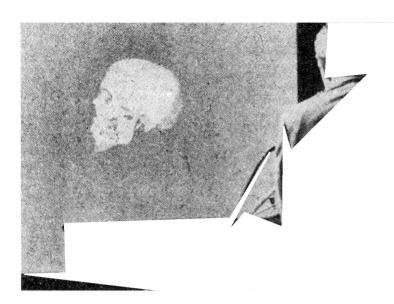

that a library is a public building '... where knowledge is collected, stored and made accessible...' and that 'this knowledge ... [allows] people to develop a degree of historical and social awareness'.[11] In order to explore and accentuate these two roles, he selected from his archive twelve very different motifs which allude to the library's function, location and users, while illustrating his own personal response to the building.[12] He then ordered these motifs in five thematic groups, reminiscent of the different sections of a newspaper. The group nearest ground level depict examples of man's relations to technology – and include a number of failures or dead-ends in the supposedly unchecked march of technological progress. The second group consists of reproductions of paintings representing major themes of human experience: love and eroticism, a preoccupation with the transience of life, and concentrated, contemplative study. By virtue of the origins of the paintings, the theme here could be classified as culture or art. History and politics are the focus of the next group, for which Ruff chose motifs from post-war Germany, depicting on the one hand the human urge for freedom, and on the other the consequences for the individual of totalitarianism and power-politics. The next group, in which Ruff articulates his thoughts on architecture in general and the library in particular, could, by virtue of its images and themes, also be seen as focusing on culture or science (academia). The final section deals with technology and life today, bringing the everyday lives of the students at Eberswalde into the overall scheme.

Ruff treats the facade like a pictorial broadsheet where he can present his

Newspaper Photo 014, 1990: C-Print, 16.8 x 42.4 cm

view of what is going on in and around the library, like a balladeer of old with his barrel organ and pictures. The *Newspaper Photos* are ideally suited to this purpose, since they were originally intended as illustrations for texts. Detached from their initial context, they are now able to be signifiers in a much broader sense. By allowing the images to convey a certain message, Ruff brings a hitherto neglected aspect of the archive into play, that is to say, its function as a picture store or 'visual diary'. And it is this aspect which links the content of the *Newspaper Photos* with the function and significance of the library. A library is a storehouse for knowledge – preserved in words, and supplemented by images – as well as a kind of cultural and intellectual diary of our times. The newspaper photographs on the facade of the library at Eberswalde are an outward, public demonstration of the library's role in maintaining the intellectual memory of the society it serves. There is a constant interchange between the inner core of the building (the books) and the outer shell (the strong external expression of a collective pictorial memory). Through this interchange all three possible premises for using the newspaper photographs – technical, aesthetic and relevance of content – are incorporated into the concept for Herzog & de Meuron's library.

With every new work, be it a new series or a multi-disciplinary collaboration, Ruff not only reflects anew on the medium and the genre he is using, but also re-assesses the function of his pictures. This regularly leads him to new pictorial conclusions, even if these involve what appears to be a complete about-turn.[13] This continual revision is possible because he takes his own pictorial ideas, rather than visible reality, as his starting point. He compares the pictures in his imagination with those that already exist in the media and in the art world, and while he is in the process of producing a series, continues to revise his own pictures until the result seems right to him. The whole focus of Ruff's work is this search for the picture – as a surface, as a composition, as an artistic construction. He allows the viewer to participate in the search, by articulating his own questions without supplying ready-made answers. With each series he seems to be employing a strategy of confusion, irritation, ambivalence, yet these are the very means by which he achieves a clearer, more precise awareness of pictures and their function.

NOTES

1   The *Newspaper Photos (Zeitungsfotos)* series was made in 1990/91 and comprises four hundred different motifs selected from the larger archive.

2   These photographs have provided the inspiration for Ruff's various *Portraits* series (1981–85, 1986–91 and 1998 to date).

3   In a conversation with the author, Ruff has said it came as a surprise to realize, one day, just how interesting he found the archive (which he stores in cardboard boxes).

4 For these works, made between 1989 and 1992, Ruff used details of images from the European Space Observatory, arranging them according to the density of the stars and the distribution of dark and light areas within them.

5 See, for example, the exh. cat. *X für U – Bilder, die lügen* (Bonn 1998) p. 22. This shows an AP photograph taken in the aftermath of the bomb attack at Thebes in Egypt on 17 November 1997, alongside a version of the same photograph, printed by the Swiss newspaper *Blick*, in which a puddle of water has been coloured red in order to dramatize reports of a 'bloodbath'.

6 '. . . Photographs are always made with a particular intention. And because they can appear so realistic and often pretend to portray reality, they are often confused with reality. . . ', Thomas Ruff, in Matthias Winzen, 'Fotografie? Ein Gespräch mit Thomas Ruff und Georg Winter', in exh. cat. *Zuspiel* (Munich/Stuttgart 1997) p. 50.

7 This would seem to be supported by the fact that each time Ruff starts a new series, his first move is to seek out photographs or other images in the genre to see how others have handled them. In addition he explores the various photographic techniques in order to make the most of their potential. During these researches he evolves his own mode of production and decides on the final look of the series.

8 Matthias Winzen, 'Memorial to the Unknown Photographer. A Conversation with Thomas Ruff', in *Das Kunst-Bulletin*, no. 3, March 1995.

9 Walter Benjamin's essay, 'The Work of Art in the Age of Mechanical Reproduction' was first published in a French translation in the *Zeitschrift für Sozialforschung*, vol. 5, 1936. The first German version was published in Benjamin's *Schriften* in 1955.

10 For more on Hans-Peter Feldmann see Werner Lippert, *Hans-Peter Feldmann/ Das Museum im Kopf* (Cologne 1989).

11 Thomas Ruff, in 'Projektbeschreibung für die Fassadengestaltung' (unpublished).

12 With one exception, however, he did not select previously finished pictures from the above-mentioned series, instead choosing others that were still in his archive.

13 As illustrated by the series of *Nudes* (since 1999), for which Ruff has been digitally manipulating pornographic photos from the Internet, in certain cases working with extremely blurred images – a departure from his concern with producing absolutely sharp, precise photos, first evident in his *Portraits*.